Fifth Edition

QUICK
JOB SEARCH

Seven Steps to Getting a Good Job in Less Time

Michael Farr

Contents

Step 1: Identify Your Key Skills and Develop a "Skills Language" to Describe Yourself.. 1

Step 2: Define Your Ideal Job 7

Step 3: Use the Most Effective Methods to Find a Job in Less Time 20

Step 4: Write a Simple Resume Now and a Better One Later............... 31

Step 5: Organize Your Time to Get Two Interviews a Day 48

Step 6: Dramatically Improve Your Interviewing Skills........................... 51

Step 7: Follow Up on All Job Leads 55

Appendix A: Essential Job Search Data Worksheet............................. 59

Appendix B: Additional Resources 67

Appendix C: Use a Career Portfolio to Support Your Resume 71

jist *Works*
America's Career Publisher®

Quick Job Search, Fifth Edition

© 2010 by JIST Publishing

Published by JIST Works, an imprint of JIST Publishing
7321 Shadeland Station, Suite 200
Indianapolis, IN 46256-3923
Phone: 800-648-JIST   Fax: 877-454-7839   E-mail: info@jist.com

Visit our Web site at **www.jist.com** for information on JIST, tables of contents, sample pages, and ordering instructions for our many products!

Note to instructors: Free instructor's tips are available at www.jist.com. An instructor's guide for another book, titled *Getting the Job You Really Want,* covers topics similar to those in this book and provides presentation tips, activities, and handouts. Quantity discounts are available for JIST books. Please call our Sales Department at 800-648-5478 for a free catalog and more information.

Acquisitions and Development Editor: Lori Cates Hand
Cover and Interior Designer: Aleata Halbig
Proofreader: Jeanne Clark

Printed in the United States of America
15 14 13 12 11 10   9 8 7 6 5 4 3 2

We have been careful to provide accurate information in this book, but it is possible that errors and omissions have been introduced. Please consider this in making any career plans or other important decisions. Trust your own judgment above all else and in all things.

Package of 10
ISBN: 978-1-59357-746-9

The Seven Steps for a Quick and Successful Job Search

You can't just read about getting a job. The best way to get a job is to go out and get interviews! And the best way to get interviews is to make a job out of getting a job.

After many years of experience, I have identified just seven basic things you need to do that make a big difference in your job search. Each will be covered and expanded on in this book.

1. Identify your key skills and develop a "skills language" to describe yourself.

2. Define your ideal job.

3. Use the most effective methods to find a job in less time.

4. Write a simple resume now and a better one later.

5. Organize your time to get two interviews a day.

6. Dramatically improve your interviewing skills.

7. Follow up on all leads.

So, without further delay, let's get started!

 STEP 1: Identify Your Key Skills and Develop a "Skills Language" to Describe Yourself

One survey of employers found that about 90 percent of the people they interviewed might have the required job skills, but they could not describe those skills and thereby prove that they could do the job they sought. They could not answer the basic question "Why should I hire you?"

Knowing and describing your skills is essential to doing well in interviews. This same knowledge is important to help you decide what type of job you will enjoy and do well. For these reasons, I consider identifying your skills a necessary part of a successful career plan or job search.

The Three Types of Skills

Most people think of their skills as job-related skills, such as using a computer. But we all have other types of skills that are important for success on a job—and that are important to employers. The triangle on the next page arranges skills in three groups, and I think that this is a very useful way to consider skills as you use this book, *Quick Job Search*.

Let's look at these three types of skills—self-management, transferable, and job-related—and identify those that are most important to you.

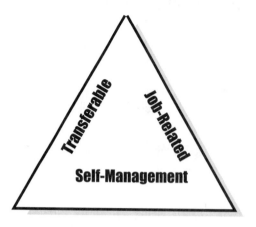

Self-Management Skills

Self-management skills (also known as adaptive skills or personality traits) are the things that make you a good worker. They describe your basic personality and your ability to adapt to new environments, as well as provide the foundation for other skills. They are some of the most important skills to emphasize in interviews, yet most job seekers don't realize their importance—and don't mention them.

Review the Self-Management Skills Checklist that follows and put a check mark beside any skills you have. The key self-management skills listed first cover abilities that employers find particularly important. If one or more of the key self-management skills apply to you, mentioning them in interviews can help you greatly.

SELF-MANAGEMENT SKILLS CHECKLIST

Following are the key self-management skills and characteristics that employers value highly. Place a check mark by those you already have.

- ❑ Honesty
- ❑ Punctuality
- ❑ Ability to follow instructions
- ❑ Ability to get along with coworkers and supervisor

- ❑ Productivity
- ❑ Good attendance
- ❑ Deadline oriented
- ❑ Hardworking

Place a check mark by other self-management skills you have.

- ❏ Ambition
- ❏ Assertiveness
- ❏ Capability
- ❏ Cheerfulness
- ❏ Competency
- ❏ Conscientiousness
- ❏ Coordination
- ❏ Creativity
- ❏ Dependability
- ❏ Discretion
- ❏ Eagerness
- ❏ Efficiency
- ❏ Energy
- ❏ Enthusiasm
- ❏ Expression
- ❏ Flexibility
- ❏ Formality
- ❏ Friendliness
- ❏ Good nature
- ❏ Helpfulness
- ❏ Humbleness

- ❏ Imagination
- ❏ Independence
- ❏ Industriousness
- ❏ Informality
- ❏ Inquisitiveness
- ❏ Intelligence
- ❏ Intuition
- ❏ Leadership
- ❏ Learning ability
- ❏ Learning oriented
- ❏ Loyalty
- ❏ Maturity
- ❏ Methodicalness
- ❏ Modesty
- ❏ Motivation
- ❏ Open-mindedness
- ❏ Optimism
- ❏ Organization
- ❏ Originality
- ❏ Patience
- ❏ Persistence

- ❏ Physical strength
- ❏ Practice
- ❏ Pride
- ❏ Problem-solving
- ❏ Reliability
- ❏ Responsibility
- ❏ Results orientation
- ❏ Self-confidence
- ❏ Self-motivation
- ❏ Sense of humor
- ❏ Sincerity
- ❏ Spontaneity
- ❏ Steadiness
- ❏ Tact
- ❏ Tenacity
- ❏ Thoroughness
- ❏ Thrift
- ❏ Trustworthiness
- ❏ Versatility

List the other self-management skills you have that are not on the list but you think are important to include.

_____

_____

_____

After you finish checking the list, circle the five skills you feel are most important for the job you want and write them in the box that follows.

YOUR TOP FIVE SELF-MANAGEMENT SKILLS

1. _____

2. _____

3. _____

4. _____

5. _____

 When thinking about their skills, some people find it helpful to complete the Essential Job Search Data Worksheet that starts on page 59. It organizes skills and accomplishments from previous jobs and other life experiences. Take a look at it and decide whether to complete it now or later.

Transferable Skills

Transferable skills are skills that can be used on more than one job. Often these skills are things that you naturally do well or that are an essential part of your personality, and are the foundations for other skills. We all have skills that can transfer from one job or career to another. For example, the ability to organize events could be used in a variety of jobs and may be essential for success in certain occupations.

Your mission is to find a job that requires the skills you have and enjoy using. But first, you need to identify your top transferable skills.

It's not bragging if it's true. Using your new skills language might be uncomfortable at first, but employers need to learn about your skills. So practice saying positive things about the skills you have for the job. If you don't, who will?

TRANSFERABLE SKILLS CHECKLIST

Following are the key transferable skills that employers value highly. Place a check mark by those you already have. You may have used them in a previous job or in some non-work setting.

- ❑ Managing money/budgets
- ❑ Speaking in public
- ❑ Managing people
- ❑ Organizing/managing projects
- ❑ Meeting deadlines
- ❑ Solving problems
- ❑ Meeting the public
- ❑ Writing well
- ❑ Negotiating
- ❑ Increasing sales or efficiency

Place a check mark by the skills you have for **working with data.**

- ❑ Analyzing data
- ❑ Auditing/checking for accuracy
- ❑ Budgeting
- ❑ Calculating/computing
- ❑ Classifying data
- ❑ Comparing/evaluating
- ❑ Compiling/recording facts
- ❑ Counting/taking inventory
- ❑ Investigating
- ❑ Keeping financial records
- ❑ Observing/inspecting
- ❑ Paying attention to details
- ❑ Researching/locating information
- ❑ Synthesizing

Place a check mark by the skills you have for **working with people.**

- ❑ Administering
- ❑ Being diplomatic and tactful
- ❑ Being kind
- ❑ Being outgoing
- ❑ Being patient
- ❑ Being sensitive and empathetic
- ❑ Being sociable
- ❑ Caring for others
- ❑ Coaching
- ❑ Confronting others
- ❑ Counseling people
- ❑ Demonstrating
- ❑ Handling criticism
- ❑ Having insight
- ❑ Helping others
- ❑ Instructing/teaching others
- ❑ Interviewing people
- ❑ Listening
- ❑ Persuading
- ❑ Supervising
- ❑ Tolerating
- ❑ Trusting
- ❑ Understanding

(continued)

(continued)

Place a check mark by your skills in **working with words and ideas.**

❏ Being articulate
❏ Being inventive
❏ Being logical
❏ Communicating verbally
❏ Corresponding with others
❏ Creating new ideas
❏ Designing

❏ Editing
❏ Reasoning
❏ Remembering information
❏ Researching information
❏ Speaking publicly
❏ Writing clearly

Place a check mark by the **leadership skills** you have.

❏ Being competitive
❏ Delegating
❏ Directing others
❏ Explaining concepts
❏ Getting results
❏ Having self-confidence
❏ Influencing others
❏ Making decisions

❏ Mediating problems
❏ Motivating people
❏ Motivating yourself
❏ Negotiating agreements
❏ Planning
❏ Running meetings
❏ Solving problems
❏ Taking risks

Place a check mark by your **creative or artistic skills.**

❏ Appreciating music
❏ Creating, inventing
❏ Dancing
❏ Drawing, painting
❏ Expressing yourself artistically

❏ Performing/acting
❏ Playing instruments
❏ Presenting artistic ideas
❏ Writing creatively

Place a check mark by your skills for **working with things.**

❏ Assembling or making things
❏ Building, observing, and inspecting things
❏ Constructing or repairing things

❏ Driving or operating vehicles
❏ Operating tools/machines
❏ Using your hands

Add the other transferable skills you have that have not been mentioned but you think are important to include.

_____

_____

_____

When you are finished, circle the five transferable skills you feel are most important for you to use in your next job and list them below.

YOUR TOP FIVE TRANSFERABLE SKILLS

1. _____

2. _____

3. _____

4. _____

5. _____

Job-Related Skills

Job-content or job-related skills are those you need to do a particular occupation. A carpenter, for example, needs to know how to use various tools. Before you select job-related skills to emphasize, you must first have a clear idea of the jobs you want. So let's put off developing your job-related skills list until you have defined the job you want—the topic that is covered next.

STEP 2: Define Your Ideal Job

Too many people look for a job without clearly knowing what they are looking for. Before you go out seeking a job, I suggest that you first define exactly what you want—not just *a job* but *the job*.

Most people think that a job objective is the same as a job title, but it isn't. You need to consider other elements of what makes a job satisfying for you. Then, later, you can decide what that job is called and what industry it might be in. You can compromise on what you consider your ideal job later if you need to.

EIGHT FACTORS TO CONSIDER IN DEFINING YOUR IDEAL JOB

As you try to define your ideal job, consider the following eight important questions. When you know what you want, your task then becomes finding a position that is as close to your ideal job as possible.

1. **What skills do you want to use?** From the skills lists in Step 1, select the top five skills that you enjoy using and most want to use in your next job.

   a. _____

   b. _____

   c. _____

   d. _____

   e. _____

2. **What type of special knowledge do you have?** Perhaps you know how to fix radios, keep accounting records, or cook food. Write down the things you know from schooling, training, hobbies, family experiences, and other sources. One or more of these knowledge areas could make you a very desirable applicant in the right setting.

   _____

   _____

3. **With what types of people do you prefer to work?** Do you like to work with competitive people, or do you prefer hardworking folks, creative personalities, relaxed people, or some other types?

   _____

   _____

4. **What type of work environment do you prefer?** Do you want to work inside, outside, in a quiet place, in a busy place, or in a clean or messy place; or do you want to have a window with a nice view? List the types of environments you prefer.

   _____

   _____

5. **Where do you want your next job to be located—in what city or region?** If you are open to living and working anywhere, what would your ideal community be like? Near a bus line? Close to a childcare center?

_____

_____

6. **What benefits or income do you hope to have in your next job?** Many people will take less money or fewer benefits if they like a job in other ways—or if they need a job quickly to survive. Think about the minimum you would take as well as what you would eventually like to earn. Your next job will probably pay somewhere in between.

_____

_____

7. **How much and what types of responsibility are you willing to accept?** Usually, the more money you want to make, the more responsibility you must accept. Do you want to work by yourself, be part of a group, or be in charge? If you want to be in charge, how many people are you willing to supervise?

_____

_____

8. **What values are important or have meaning to you?** Do you have important values you would prefer to include in considering the work you do? For example, some people want to work to help others, clean up the environment, build structures, make machines work, gain power or prestige, or care for animals or plants. Think about what is important to you and how you might include this in your next job.

_____

_____

_____

Is It Possible to Find Your Ideal Job?

Can you find a job that meets all the criteria you just defined? Perhaps. Some people do. The harder you look, the more likely you are to find it. But you will likely need to compromise, so it is useful to know what is *most* important to include in your next job. Go back over your responses to the eight factors and mark a few of those that you would most like to have in your ideal job.

FACTORS I WANT IN MY IDEAL JOB

Write a brief description of your ideal job. Don't worry about a job title, whether you have the necessary experience, or other practical matters yet.

_____

_____

_____

How Can You Explore Specific Job Titles and Industries?

You might find your ideal job in an occupation you haven't considered yet. And, even if you are sure of the occupation you want, it may be in an industry that is unfamiliar to you. This combination of occupation and industry forms the basis for your job search, and you should consider a variety of options.

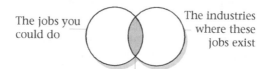

The jobs you could do   The industries where these jobs exist

Your ideal job exists in the overlap of those jobs that interest you most *and* in those industries that best meet your needs and interests!

There are thousands of job titles, and many jobs are highly specialized, employing just a few people. Although one of these more specialized jobs might be just what you want, most work falls within more general job titles that employ large numbers of people.

REVIEW THE TOP JOBS IN THE WORKFORCE

The list of job titles that follows was based on a list developed by the U.S. Department of Labor. It contains 289 major jobs that employ about 88 percent of the U.S. workforce.

The job titles are organized within 16 major groupings called interest areas, presented in all capital letters and bold type. These groupings will help you quickly identify fields most likely to interest you. Job titles are presented in regular type within these groupings.

Begin with the interest areas that appeal to you most, and underline any job title that interests you. (Don't worry for now about whether you have the experience or credentials to do these jobs.) Then quickly review the remaining interest areas, underlining any job titles there that interest you. Note that some job titles are listed more than once because they fit into more than one interest area. When you have gone through all 16 interest areas, go back and circle the 5 to 10 job titles that interest you most. These are the ones you will want to research in more detail.

1. **AGRICULTURE, FOOD, AND NATURAL RESOURCES:** Agricultural and Food Scientists; Agricultural Workers; Animal Care and Service Workers; Conservation Scientists and Foresters; Environmental Scientists and Specialists; Farmers, Ranchers, and Agricultural Managers; Fishers and Fishing Vessel Operators; Floral Designers; Food Processing Occupations; Forest and Conservation Workers; Graders and Sorters, Agricultural Products; Grounds Maintenance Workers; Logging Workers; Pest Control Workers; Recreation Workers; Veterinarians; Water and Liquid Waste Treatment Plant and System Operators.

2. **ARCHITECTURE AND CONSTRUCTION:** Architects, Except Landscape and Naval; Boilermakers; Brickmasons, Blockmasons, and Stonemasons; Carpenters; Carpet, Floor, and Tile Installers and Finishers; Cement Masons, Concrete Finishers, Segmental Pavers, and Terrazzo Workers; Construction and Building Inspectors; Construction Equipment Operators; Construction Laborers; Construction Managers; Cost Estimators; Drafters; Drywall and Ceiling Tile Installers, Tapers, Plasterers, and Stucco Masons; Electricians; Glaziers; Heating, Air-Conditioning, and Refrigeration Mechanics and

(continued)

(continued)

Installers; Home Appliance Repairers; Insulation Workers; Interior Designers; Landscape Architects; Line Installers and Repairers; Painters and Paperhangers; Plumbers, Pipelayers, Pipefitters, and Steamfitters; Roofers; Structural and Reinforcing Iron and Metal Workers; Surveyors, Cartographers, Photogrammetrists, and Surveying and Mapping Technicians.

3. **ARTS, AUDIO/VIDEO TECHNOLOGY, AND COMMUNICATIONS:** Actors, Producers, and Directors; Announcers; Archivists, Curators, and Museum Technicians; Artists and Related Workers; Authors, Writers, and Editors; Broadcast and Sound Engineering Technicians and Radio Operators; Commercial and Industrial Designers; Communications Equipment Operators; Dancers and Choreographers; Electronic Home Entertainment Equipment Installers and Repairers; Fashion Designers; Graphic Designers; Interior Designers; Musicians, Singers, and Related Workers; News Analysts, Reporters, and Correspondents; Photographers; Photographic Process Workers and Processing Machine Operators; Prepress Technicians and Workers; Public Relations Specialists; Radio and Telecommunications Equipment Installers and Repairers; Technical Writers; Television, Video, and Motion Picture Camera Operators and Editors.

4. **BUSINESS, MANAGEMENT, AND ADMINISTRATION:** Accountants and Auditors; Administrative Services Managers; Advertising, Marketing, Promotions, Public Relations, and Sales Managers; Advertising Sales Agents; Billing and Posting Clerks and Machine Operators; Bookkeeping, Accounting, and Auditing Clerks; Brokerage Clerks; Budget Analysts; Couriers and Messengers; Customer Service Representatives; Data Entry and Information Processing Workers; Desktop Publishers; Economists; File Clerks; Financial Analysts; Financial Managers; Human Resources Assistants, Except Payroll and Timekeeping; Human Resources, Training, and Labor Relations Managers and Specialists; Interviewers, Except Eligibility and Loan; Management Analysts; Office and Administrative Support Supervisors and Managers; Office Clerks, General; Operations Research Analysts; Order Clerks; Payroll and Timekeeping Clerks; Procurement

Clerks; Purchasing Managers, Buyers, and Purchasing Agents; Receptionists and Information Clerks; Secretaries and Administrative Assistants; Shipping, Receiving, and Traffic Clerks; Statisticians; Top Executives; Weighers, Measurers, Checkers, and Samplers, Recordkeeping.

5. **EDUCATION AND TRAINING:** Athletes, Coaches, Umpires, and Related Workers; Counselors; Education Administrators; Fitness Workers; Instructional Coordinators; Interpreters and Translators; Librarians; Library Technicians and Library Assistants; Recreation Workers; Teacher Assistants; Teachers—Adult Literacy and Remedial Education; Teachers—Kindergarten, Elementary, Middle, and Secondary; Teachers—Postsecondary; Teachers—Preschool, Except Special Education; Teachers—Self-Enrichment Education; Teachers— Special Education; Teachers—Vocational.

6. **FINANCE:** Actuaries; Bill and Account Collectors; Budget Analysts; Claims Adjusters, Appraisers, Examiners, and Investigators; Credit Authorizers, Checkers, and Clerks; Financial Analysts; Financial Managers; Insurance Sales Agents; Insurance Underwriters; Loan Interviewers and Clerks; Loan Officers; Personal Financial Advisors; Securities, Commodities, and Financial Services Sales Agents; Tellers.

7. **GOVERNMENT AND PUBLIC ADMINISTRATION:** Accountants and Auditors; Administrative Services Managers; Sociologists and Political Scientists; Tax Examiners, Collectors, and Revenue Agents; Top Executives; Urban and Regional Planners.

8. **HEALTH SCIENCE:** Audiologists; Cardiovascular Technologists and Technicians; Chiropractors; Clinical Laboratory Technologists and Technicians; Counselors; Dental Assistants; Dental Hygienists; Dentists; Diagnostic Medical Sonographers; Dietitians and Nutritionists; Emergency Medical Technicians and Paramedics; Health Educators; Home Health Aides and Personal and Home Care Aides; Licensed Practical and Licensed Vocational Nurses; Massage Therapists; Medical and Health Services Managers; Medical Assistants; Medical, Dental, and Ophthalmic Laboratory Technicians; Medical Records and Health Information Technicians; Medical Scientists;

(continued)

(continued)

Medical Transcriptionists; Nuclear Medicine Technologists; Nursing and Psychiatric Aides; Occupational Therapist Assistants and Aides; Occupational Therapists; Opticians, Dispensing; Optometrists; Pharmacists; Pharmacy Technicians and Aides; Physical Therapist Assistants and Aides; Physical Therapists; Physician Assistants; Physicians and Surgeons; Podiatrists; Psychologists; Radiation Therapists; Radiologic Technologists and Technicians; Recreational Therapists; Registered Nurses; Respiratory Therapists; Respiratory Therapy Technicians; Speech-Language Pathologists; Surgical Technologists.

9. **HOSPITALITY AND TOURISM:** Building Cleaning Workers; Chefs, Head Cooks, and Food Preparation and Serving Supervisors; Cooks and Food Preparation Workers; Food and Beverage Serving and Related Workers; Food Service Managers; Lodging Managers; Reservation and Transportation Ticket Agents and Travel Clerks; Travel Agents.

10. **HUMAN SERVICE:** Barbers, Cosmetologists, and Other Personal Appearance Workers; Child Care Workers; Counselors; Eligibility Interviewers, Government Programs; Epidemiologists; Funeral Directors; Health Educators; Interpreters and Translators; Probation Officers and Correctional Treatment Specialists; Psychologists; Recreation Workers; Social Workers; Sociologists and Political Scientists.

11. **INFORMATION TECHNOLOGY:** Computer and Information Systems Managers; Computer Control Programmers and Operators; Computer Network, Systems, and Database Administrators; Computer Operators; Computer Scientists; Computer Software Engineers and Computer Programmers; Computer Support Specialists; Computer Systems Analysts.

12. **LAW, PUBLIC SAFETY, CORRECTIONS, AND SECURITY:** Correctional Officers; Court Reporters; Fire Fighters; Fire Inspectors and Investigators; Judges, Magistrates, and Other Judicial Workers; Lawyers; Paralegals and Legal Assistants; Police and Detectives; Police, Fire, and Ambulance Dispatchers; Private Detectives and

Investigators; Science Technicians; Security Guards and Gaming Surveillance Officers.

13. **MANUFACTURING:** Assemblers and Fabricators; Cost Estimators; Electrical and Electronics Installers and Repairers; Elevator Installers and Repairers; Industrial Machinery Mechanics and Millwrights; Inspectors, Testers, Sorters, Samplers, and Weighers; Jewelers and Precious Stone and Metal Workers; Line Installers and Repairers; Machine Setters, Operators, and Tenders—Metal and Plastic; Machinists; Occupational Health and Safety Specialists; Painting and Coating Workers, Except Construction and Maintenance; Power Plant Operators, Distributors, and Dispatchers; Semiconductor Processors; Sheet Metal Workers; Stationary Engineers and Boiler Operators; Textile, Apparel, and Furnishings Occupations; Tool and Die Makers; Watch Repairers; Welding, Soldering, and Brazing Workers; Woodworkers.

14. **MARKETING, SALES, AND SERVICE:** Advertising, Marketing, Promotions, Public Relations, and Sales Managers; Appraisers and Assessors of Real Estate; Cashiers; Counter and Rental Clerks; Demonstrators and Product Promoters; Market and Survey Researchers; Models; Real Estate Brokers and Sales Agents; Retail Salespersons; Sales Engineers; Sales Representatives, Wholesale and Manufacturing; Sales Worker Supervisors; Stock Clerks and Order Fillers.

15. **SCIENCE, TECHNOLOGY, ENGINEERING, AND MATHEMATICS:** Atmospheric Scientists; Biological Scientists; Chemists and Materials Scientists; Computer Software Engineers and Computer Programmers; Drafters; Engineering and Natural Sciences Managers; Engineering Technicians; Engineers; Epidemiologists; Geoscientists and Hydrologists; Mathematicians; Medical Scientists; Operations Research Analysts; Physicists and Astronomers; Psychologists; Science Technicians; Sociologists and Political Scientists; Statisticians.

(continued)

(continued)

16. **TRANSPORTATION, DISTRIBUTION, AND LOGISTICS:** Air Traffic Controllers; Aircraft and Avionics Equipment Mechanics and Service Technicians; Aircraft Pilots and Flight Engineers; Automotive Body and Related Repairers; Automotive Service Technicians and Mechanics; Bus Drivers; Diesel Service Technicians and Mechanics; Material Moving Occupations; Production, Planning, and Expediting Clerks; Rail Transportation Occupations; Shipping, Receiving, and Traffic Clerks; Small Engine Mechanics; Taxi Drivers and Chauffeurs; Truck Drivers and Driver/Sales Workers; Water Transportation Occupations.

You can find thorough descriptions for the job titles in the preceding list in the Occupational Outlook Handbook, *published by the U.S. Department of Labor. Its descriptions include information on earnings, training and education needed to hold specific jobs, working conditions, advancement opportunities, projected growth, and sources for additional information. Most libraries have this book.*

You also can find descriptions of these jobs on the Internet. Go to www.bls.gov/oco/.

The New Guide for Occupational Exploration *also provides more information on the interest areas and jobs used in this list. This book is published by JIST Publishing and describes more than 900 major jobs, arranged within groupings of related jobs.*

Finally, Appendix B, "Additional Resources," in this book gives you resources for more job information.

CONSIDER MAJOR INDUSTRIES

What industry you work in is often as important as the career field. For example, some industries pay much better than others, and others may simply be more interesting to you. A book titled *40 Best Fields for Your Career* contains very helpful reviews for each of the major industries mentioned in the following list. Many libraries and bookstores carry this book, as well as the U.S. Department of Labor's *Career Guide to Industries,* or you can find the information on the Internet at www.bls.gov/oco/cg/.

Underline industries that interest you, and then learn more about the opportunities they present. Jobs in most careers are available in a variety of industries, so consider what industries fit you best and focus your job search in these.

Agriculture, and natural resources: Agriculture, forestry, and fishing; mining; oil and gas extraction.

Manufacturing, construction, and utilities: Aerospace product and parts manufacturing; chemical manufacturing, except drugs; computer and electronic product manufacturing; food manufacturing; machinery manufacturing; motor vehicle and parts manufacturing; pharmaceutical and medicine manufacturing; printing; steel manufacturing; textile, textile products, and apparel manufacturing; utilities.

Trade: Automobile dealers; clothing, accessories, and general merchandise stores; grocery stores; wholesale trade.

Transportation: Air transportation; truck transportation and warehousing.

Information: Broadcasting; Internet service providers, Web search portals, and data-processing services; motion picture and video industries; publishing, except software; software publishing; telecommunications.

Financial activities: Banking; insurance; securities, commodities, and other investments.

Professional and business services: Advertising and public relations; computer systems design and related services; employment services; management, scientific, and technical consulting services; scientific research and development services.

Education, health care, and social services: Child daycare services; educational services; health care; social assistance, except child care.

Leisure and Hospitality: Art, entertainment, and recreation; food services and drinking places; hotels and other accommodations.

Government and advocacy, grantmaking, and civic organizations: Advocacy, grantmaking, and civic organizations; federal government; state and local government, except education and health care.

THE TOP JOBS AND INDUSTRIES THAT INTEREST YOU

Go back over the lists of job titles and industries. For numbers 1 and 2 below, list the jobs that interest you most. Then select the industries that interest you most, and list them below in number 3. These are the jobs and industries you should research most carefully. Your ideal job is likely to be found in some combination of these jobs and industries, or in more specialized but related jobs and industries. Put a star next to the one you like best.

1. The five job titles that interest you most

   a. _____

   b. _____

   c. _____

   d. _____

   e. _____

2. The five next-most-interesting job titles

   a. _____

   b. _____

   c. _____

   d. _____

   e. _____

3. The industries that interest you most

   a. _____

   b. _____

   c. _____

   d. _____

   e. _____

Is Self-Employment or Starting a Business an Option?

More than one in 10 workers are self-employed or own their own businesses. If these options interest you, consider them as well. Talk to people in similar roles to gather information, and look for books and Web sites that provide information on options that are similar to those that interest you. Examples of jobs with high percentages of self-employed workers include

- ❑ Farmers and ranchers
- ❑ Multimedia artists and animators
- ❑ Copywriters
- ❑ Poets, lyricists, and creative writers
- ❑ Massage therapists
- ❑ Real estate brokers

The Small Business Administration's Web site at www.sba.gov is a good source of basic information on starting your own business.

SELF-EMPLOYMENT AREAS OF INTEREST

In the following space, write your current interest in self-employment or starting a business in an area related to your general job objective.

Are you interested in working for yourself? _____

What types of businesses are related to the jobs that interest you most?

_____

_____

Who can you talk with to get more information about what it's like to be self-employed in this field? _____

_____

Identify Your Job-Related Skills for Your Ideal Job

Back on page 7, I suggested that you should first define the job you want and then identify key job-related skills you have that support your ability to do that job. These are the job-related skills to emphasize in interviews.

So, now that you have determined your ideal job (the one you put a star next to on page 18), you can pinpoint the job-related skills it requires. If you haven't done so, complete the Essential Job Search Data Worksheet on pages 59–65. Completing it will give you specific skills and accomplishments to highlight. Look up your ideal job at http://online.onetcenter.org/. See which skills are required for this job. Then see how many of those overlap with the skills you have.

Yes, completing that worksheet requires time, but doing so will help you clearly define key skills to emphasize in interviews—when what you say matters so much. People who complete that worksheet will do better in their interviews than those who don't. After you complete the Essential Job Search Data Worksheet, you are ready to list your top five job-related skills.

YOUR TOP FIVE JOB-RELATED SKILLS

List the five job-related skills you think are most important. Include the job-related skills you have that you would most like to use in your next job.

1. _____

2. _____

3. _____

4. _____

5. _____

STEP 3: Use the Most Effective Methods to Find a Job in Less Time

Employer surveys have found that most employers don't advertise their job openings. They most often hire people they already know, people who find out about the jobs through word of mouth, or people who happen to be in the right place at the right time. Although luck plays a part in finding job openings, you can use the tips in this step to increase your luck.

Most job seekers don't know how ineffective some traditional job hunting techniques tend to be. For example, the chart below shows that fewer than 15 percent of all job seekers get jobs from the newspaper want ads, most of which also appear online. Other traditional techniques include using public and private employment agencies, filling out paper and electronic applications, and mailing or e-mailing unsolicited resumes.

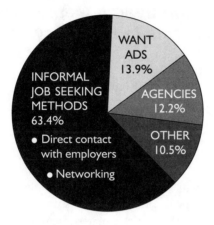

How people find jobs.

Informal, nontraditional job seeking methods have a much larger success rate. These methods are active rather than passive and include making direct contact with employers and networking.

The truth is that every job search method works for someone. But experience and research show that some methods are more effective than others are. Your task in the job search is to spend more of your time using more effective methods—and increase the effectiveness of all the methods you use. Let's start by looking at the most effective job search methods.

Use the Two Job Search Methods That Work Best

The fact is that most jobs are not advertised, so how do *you* find them? The same way that about two-thirds of all job seekers do: networking with people you know (which I call making warm contacts) and directly contacting employers (which I call making cold contacts). Both of these methods are based on the job search rule you should know above all:

The Most Important Job Search Rule: Don't wait until the job opens before contacting the employer!

Employers fill most jobs with people they meet before a job is formally open. The trick is to meet people who can hire you before a job is formally available. Instead of asking whether the employer has any jobs open, I suggest that you say, *"I realize you may not have any openings now, but I would still like to talk to you about the possibility of future openings."*

Most Effective Job Search Method 1: Develop a Network of Contacts in Five Easy Stages

Studies find that 40 percent of all people located their jobs through a lead provided by a friend, a relative, or an acquaintance. That makes the people you know your number one source of job leads—more effective than all the traditional methods combined! Developing and using your contacts is called *networking,* and here's how it works:

1. **Make lists of people you know.** Make a thorough list of anyone you are friendly with. Then make a separate list of all your relatives. These two lists alone often add up to 25 to 100 people or more. Next, think of other groups of people that you have something in common with, such as former coworkers or classmates, members of your social or sports groups, members of your professional association, former employers, neighbors, and other groups. You might not know many of these people personally or well, but most will help you if you ask them. An easy way to find networking contacts is to join an online networking site such as LinkedIn (www.linkedin.com).

2. **Contact each person in your list in a systematic way.** Obviously, some people will be more helpful than others, but any one of them might help you find a job lead.

3. **Present yourself well.** Begin with your friends and relatives. Call and tell them you are looking for a job and need their help. Be as clear as possible about the type of employment you want and the skills and qualifications you have. Look at the sample JIST Card and phone script later in this step for good presentation ideas.

4. **Ask your contacts for leads.** It is possible that your contacts will know of a job opening that interests you. If so, get the details and get right on it! More likely, however, they will not, so you should ask each person the Three Magic Networking Questions.

The Three Magic Networking Questions

- **Do you know of any openings for a person with my skills?**

  If the answer is "No" (which it usually is), then ask...

- **Do you know of someone else who might know of such an opening?**

  If your contact does, get that name and ask for another one. If he or she doesn't, ask...

- **Do you know of anyone who might know of someone else who might know of a job opening?**

  Another good way to ask this is "Do you know someone who knows lots of people?" If all else fails, this will usually get you a name.

5. **Contact these referrals and ask them the same questions.** From each person you contact, try to get two names of other people you might contact. Doing this consistently can extend your network of acquaintances by hundreds of people. Eventually, one of these people will hire you or refer you to someone who will!

If you are persistent in following these five steps, networking might be the only job search method you need. It works.

Most Effective Job Search Method 2: Contact Employers Directly

It takes more courage, but making direct contact with employers is a very effective job search technique. I call these "cold contacts" because people you don't know in advance will need to warm up to your inquiries. Two basic techniques for making cold contacts follow.

Use the yellow pages to find potential employers. Begin by looking at the index in the front of your phone book's yellow pages. For each entry, ask yourself, "Would an organization of this kind need a person with my skills?" If you answer "Yes," then that organization or business type is a possible target. You can also rate "Yes" entries based on your interest, writing a "1" next to those that seem very interesting, a "2" next to those that you are not sure of, and a "3" next to those that aren't interesting at all.

Next, select a type of organization that got a "Yes" response and turn to that section of the yellow pages. Call each organization listed there and ask to speak to the person who is most likely to hire or supervise you—typically the manager of the business or a department head—not the personnel or human resources manager. A sample telephone script is included later in this section to give you ideas about what to say.

You can easily adapt this approach for use on the Internet by using sites such as www.yellowpages.com to get contacts anywhere in the world, or you can find phone and e-mail contacts on an employer's own Web site.

Drop in without an appointment. Another effective cold contact method is to just walk into a business or organization that interests you and ask to speak to the person in charge. Although dropping in is particularly effective in small businesses, it also works surprisingly well in larger ones. Remember to ask for an interview even if there are no openings now. If your timing is inconvenient, ask for a better time to come back for an interview.

Most Jobs Are with Small Employers

Businesses and organizations with fewer than 250 employees employ half of all workers and create more than 75 percent of all new jobs each year. They are simply too important to overlook in your job search! Many of them don't have personnel departments, which makes direct contacts even easier and more effective.

Create a Powerful Job Search Tool: The JIST Card®

Look at the sample cards that follow. They are JIST Cards, and they get results. They can be computer printed or even neatly written on a 3-by-5–inch card. JIST Cards include the essential information employers want to know.

A JIST Card Is a Mini Resume

JIST Cards have been used by thousands of job search programs and millions of people. Employers like their direct and timesaving format, and they have been proven as an effective tool to get job leads. Attach one to your resume. Give them to friends, relatives, and other contacts and ask them to pass them along to others who might know of an opening. Enclose them in thank-you notes after interviews. Leave one with employers as a business card. However you get them in circulation, you may be surprised at how well they work.

You can easily create JIST Cards on a computer and print them on card stock you can buy at any office-supply store. Or you can have a few hundred printed cheaply by a local quick-print shop. Although they are often done as 3-by-5 cards, they can be printed in any size or format, including standard business card size.

Sandy Nolan

Position: General Office/Clerical

Cell phone: (512) 232-9213

Email: snolan@aol.com

More than two years of work experience plus one year of training in office practices. Type 55 wpm, trained in word processing, post general ledger, have good interpersonal skills, and get along with most people. Can meet deadlines and handle pressure well.

Willing to work any hours.

Organized, honest, reliable, and hardworking.

Richard Straightarrow   Home: (602) 253-9678
                                              Cell: (602) 257-6643
                                          E-mail: RSS@email.com

Objective: **Electronics installation, maintenance, and sales**

Four years of work experience plus a two-year A.S. degree in Electronics Engineering Technology. Managed a $360K annual business while attending school full time, with grades in the top 25%. Familiar with all major electronic diagnostic and repair equipment. Hands-on experience with medical, consumer, communication, and industrial electronics equipment and applications. Good problem-solving and communication skills. Customer service oriented.

Willing to do what it takes to get the job done.

Self-motivated, dependable, learn quickly.

A JIST Card Can Lead to an Effective Phone Script

The phone is an essential job search tool that can get you more interviews per hour than any other method. But the technique won't work unless you use it actively throughout your search. After you have created your JIST Card, you can use it as the basis for a phone script to make warm or cold calls. Revise your JIST Card content so that it sounds natural when spoken, and then edit it until you can read it out loud in about 30 seconds. The sample phone script that follows is based on the content of a JIST Card. Use it to help you modify your own JIST Card into a phone script.

"Hello. My name is Pam Nykanen. I am interested in a position in hotel management. I have four years of experience in sales, catering, and accounting with a 300-room hotel. I also have an associate degree in hotel management, plus one year of experience with the Brady Culinary Institute. During my employment, I helped double revenues from meetings and conferences and increased bar revenues by 46 percent. I have good problem-solving skills and am good with people. I am also well-organized, hardworking, and detail-oriented. When may I come in to talk with you about opportunities in your organization?"

With your script in hand, make some practice calls to warm or cold contacts. If making cold calls, contact the person most likely to supervise you. Then present your script just as you practiced it—without stopping.

Although the sample script assumes that you are calling someone you don't know, you can change it to address warm contacts and referrals. Making cold calls takes courage but works very well for many who are willing to do it.

Use the Internet in Your Job Search

The Internet has limitations as a job search tool. While many have used it to get job leads, it has not worked well for far more. Too many assume they can simply add their resume to resume databases and employers will line up to hire them. Just like the older approach of sending out lots of resumes, good things sometimes happen, but not often.

I recommend two points that apply to all job search methods, including using the Internet:

- It is unwise to rely on just one or two methods in conducting your job search.

- It is essential that you use an active rather than a passive approach in your job search.

Use More Than One Job Search Method

I encourage you to use the Internet in your job search, but I suggest that you use it along with other techniques. Use the same sorts of job search techniques online as you do offline, including contacting employers directly and building up a network of personal contacts that can help you with your search.

Tips to Increase Your Effectiveness in Internet Job Searches

The following tips can increase the effectiveness of using the Internet in your job search:

- **Be as specific as possible in the job you seek.** This is important in using any job search method, and it's even more important in using the Internet in your job search. The Internet is enormous, so it is essential to be as focused as possible in your search. Narrow your job title or titles to be as specific as possible. Limit your search to specific industries or areas of specialization. Locate and use specialized job banks in your area of interest.

- **Have reasonable expectations.** Success on the Internet is more likely if you understand its limitations and strengths. For example, employers trying to find someone with skills in high demand, such as nurses, are more likely to use the Internet to recruit job candidates.

- **Limit your geographic options.** If you don't want to move or would move only to certain areas, state this preference on your resume and restrict your search to those areas. Many Internet sites allow you to view or search for only those jobs that meet your location criteria.

- **Create an electronic resume.** With few exceptions, resumes submitted to Internet resume databases end up as simple text files with no graphic elements. Employers search these databases for resumes that include keywords or meet other searchable criteria. So create a simple text resume for Internet use and include words that are likely to be used by employers searching for someone with your abilities. (See Step 4 for more on creating an electronic resume or online portfolio.)

- **Get your resume into the major resume databases.** Most Internet employment sites let you add your resume for free and then charge employers to advertise openings or to search for candidates. Although adding your resume to these databases is not likely to result in job offers, doing so allows you to use your stored resume to easily apply for positions that are posted at these sites. These easy-to-use sites often provide all sorts of useful information for job seekers.

- **Make direct contacts.** Visit the Web sites of organizations that interest you and learn more about them. Many post openings, allow you to apply online, offer information on benefits and work environment, or even provide access to staff who can answer your questions. Even if they don't, you can always search the site or e-mail a request for the name of the person in charge of the work that interests you and then communicate with that person directly.

- **Network.** You can network online, too, finding names and e-mail addresses of potential employer contacts or of other people who might know someone with job openings. The best place to start your online networking is LinkedIn (www.linkedin.com). Twitter (www.twitter.com) is also a powerful online networking tool, and you can even find some good leads among your Facebook friends. In addition, look at and participate in interest groups, professional association sites, alumni sites, chat rooms, e-mail discussion lists, and employer sites—these are just some of the many creative ways to network and interact with people via the Internet.

Check Out Career-Specific Sites First

Thousands of Internet sites provide lists of job openings and information on careers or education. The best-known general job boards are CareerBuilder (www.careerbuilder.com), Monster (www.monster.com), and Yahoo! Hotjobs (http://hotjobs.yahoo.com/). Perhaps even more helpful are job aggregator sites, which pull jobs from all over the Web into one place. Two of the best-known aggregators are Indeed (www.indeed.com) and Simply Hired (www. simplyhired.com).

Get the Most Out of Less Effective Job Search Methods

Now let's look at some traditional job search methods and how you can increase their effectiveness. Only about one-third of all job seekers get their jobs using one of these methods, but you should still consider using them to some extent in your search.

Newspaper and Internet Help-Wanted Ads

Most jobs are never advertised, and fewer than 15 percent of all people get their jobs through the want ads. Everyone who reads the paper knows about these openings, so competition is fierce for the few advertised jobs.

The Internet also lists many job openings. But, as happens with newspaper ads, enormous numbers of people view these postings. Many job seekers make direct contact with employers via a company's Web site. Some people do get jobs through the bigger sites, so go ahead and apply. Just be sure to spend most of your time using more effective methods.

Filling Out Applications

Most employers require job seekers to complete a paper application form, a kiosk application on a computer at the front of the store, or an online application on the company's Web site. Applications are designed to collect negative information, and employers use applications to screen people out. If, for example, your training or work history is not the best, you will often never get an interview, even if you can do the job.

Completing applications is a more effective approach for young and entry-level job seekers. The reason is that there is usually greater need for workers for the relatively low-paying jobs typically sought by less-experienced job seekers. As a result, when employers try to fill those positions, they are more willing to accept a lack of experience or fewer job skills. Even so, you will get better results by filling out the application, if asked to do so, and then requesting an interview with the person in charge.

When you complete an application, make it neat and error free, and do not include anything that could get you screened out. If necessary, leave a problem section blank. You can always explain situations in an interview.

Public and Private Employment Agencies and Services

There are three types of employment agencies. One is operated by the government and is free. The others, private employment agencies and temp agencies, are run as for-profit businesses and charge a fee to either you or an employer. Following are the advantages and disadvantages to using each.

The government employment service and One-Stop centers. Each state and province has a network of local offices to pay unemployment compensation, provide job leads, and offer other services—at no charge to you or to employers. The service's name varies by region. It may be called Job Service, Department of Labor, Unemployment Office, Workforce Development, WorkOne, or another name. All of these offices are now online. You can find your local office at www.careeronestop.org.

The Employment and Training Administration Web site at www.doleta.gov gives you information on the programs provided by the government employment service, plus links to other useful sites.

Visit your local office early in your job search. Find out whether you qualify for unemployment compensation and learn more about its services. Look into it—the price is right.

Private employment agencies. Private employment agencies are businesses that charge a fee either to you or to the employer that hires you. Fees can be from less than one month's pay to 15 percent or more of your annual salary. You will often see these agencies' ads in the help-wanted section of the newspaper. Most have Web sites.

Be careful about using fee-based employment agencies. Recent research indicates that more people use and benefit from fee-based agencies than in the past. However, relatively few people who register with private agencies get a job through them.

If you use a private employment agency, ask for interviews with the employers who agree to pay the agency's fee. Do not sign an exclusive agreement or be pressured into accepting a job. Also, continue to actively look for your own leads. You can find these agencies in the phone book's yellow pages, and many state- or province-government Web sites offer lists of the private employment agencies in their states.

Temporary agencies. Temporary agencies offer jobs that last from several days to many months. They charge the employer an hourly fee, and then pay you a bit less and keep the difference. You pay no direct fee to the agency. Many private employment agencies now provide temporary jobs as well.

Temp agencies have grown rapidly for good reason. They provide employers with short-term help, and employers often use them to find people they might want to hire later. If the employers are dissatisfied, they can just ask the agency for different temp workers.

Temp agencies can help you survive between jobs and get experience in different work settings. Temp jobs provide a very good option while you look for long-term work, and you might get a job offer while working in a temp job. Holding a temporary job might even lead to a regular job with the same or a similar employer.

School and Other Employment Services

Only a small percentage of job seekers use school and other special employment services, probably because few job seekers have the service available to them. If you are a student or graduate, find out about any employment services at your school. Some schools provide free career counseling, resume writing help, referrals to job openings, career interest tests, reference materials, Web sites listing job openings, and other services. Special career programs work with veterans, people with disabilities, welfare recipients, union members, professional groups, and many others. So check out these services and consider using them.

Mailing Out Lots of Resumes Blindly

Many job search experts used to suggest that sending out lots of resumes was a great technique. That advice probably helped sell their resume books, but mailing resumes to people you do not know was never an effective approach. It very rarely works. A recent survey of 1,500 successful job seekers showed that only 2 percent found their positions through sending an unsolicited resume. The same is true for the Internet.

Although mailing your resume to strangers doesn't make much sense, posting it on the Internet might because

- It doesn't take much time.

- Many employers have the potential to find your resume.

- You can post your resume on niche sites that attract only employers in your field.

- Your Internet resume is easily updated, allowing you to post your current accomplishments.

- You can easily link your resume to projects and Web sites that highlight your accomplishments.

Job searching on the Internet has its limitations, just like other methods. I'll cover resumes in more detail later and provide tips on using the Internet throughout this book.

STEP 4: Write a Simple Resume Now and a Better One Later

Sending out resumes and waiting for responses is not an effective job seeking technique. But many employers *will* ask you for a resume, and it can be a useful tool in your job search. I suggest that you begin with a simple resume you can complete quickly. I've seen too many people spend weeks working on a resume when they could have been out getting interviews instead. If you want a better resume, you can work on it on weekends and evenings. So let's begin with the basics.

The following tips make sense for any resume format:

- **Write it yourself.** It's okay to look at other resumes for ideas, but write yours yourself. Doing so will force you to organize your thoughts and background.

- **Make it error free.** One spelling or grammar error will create a negative impression. Get someone else to review your final draft for any errors. Then review it again because these rascals have a way of slipping in.

- **Make it look good.** Poor copy quality, cheap paper, bad type quality, or anything else that creates a poor appearance will turn off employers to even the best resume content. Get professional help with design and printing if necessary. Many professional resume writers and even print shops offer writing and desktop design services if you need help.

- **Be brief, be relevant.** Many good resumes fit on one page, and few justify more than two. Include only the most important points. Use short sentences and action words. If it doesn't relate to and support the job objective, cut it!

- **Be honest.** Don't overstate your qualifications. If you end up getting a job you can't handle, who does it help? And a lie can result in your being fired later.

- **Be positive.** Emphasize your accomplishments and results. A resume is no place to be too humble or to display your faults.

- **Be specific.** Instead of saying, "I am good with people," say, "I supervised four people in the warehouse and increased productivity by 30 percent." Use numbers whenever possible, such as the number of people served, percentage of sales increase, or amount of dollars saved.

Get Your Resume Online

Employers may ask you to send them your resume online. Pay attention to their instructions, because they will probably specify whether they want you to send your Word file as an attachment, send a PDF, or transmit a plain-text resume via e-mail or their Web site. Louise Kursmark, coauthor of *15-Minute Cover Letter,* provides these steps for converting your resume to plain text:

1. Save your resume with a different name and select "text only," "ASCII," or "Plain Text (*.txt)" in the "Save As Type" option box.

2. Reopen the file. Your word processor has automatically reformatted your resume into Courier font, removed all formatting, and left-justified the text.

3. Reset the margins to 2 inches left and right, so that you have a narrow column of text rather than a full-page width. Adjust line lengths to fit within the narrow margins by adding hard returns.

4. Fix any glitches such as odd characters that may have been inserted to take the place of "curly" quotes, dashes, accents, or other nonstandard symbols.

5. Remove any tabs and adjust spacing as necessary. You might add a few extra blank spaces, move text down to the next line, or add extra blank lines for readability.

6. Consider adding horizontal dividers to break the resume into sections. You can use a row of any standard typewriter symbols, such as *, -, (,), =, +, ^, or #.

When you close the file, it will be saved with the .txt file extension. When you are ready to use it, just open the file, select and copy the text, and paste it into the online application or e-mail message.

Never delay or slow down your job search because your resume is not good enough. The best approach is to create a simple and acceptable resume as quickly as possible and then use it. As time permits, create a better one if you feel you must.

Writing Chronological Resumes

Most resumes use a chronological format where the most recent experience is listed first, followed by each preceding job. Most employers prefer this format. It works fine for someone with work experience in several similar jobs, but not as well for those with limited experience or for career changers.

Look at the two resumes for Judith Jones that follow. Both use the chronological approach.

The first resume would work fine for most job search needs. It could be completed in about an hour. Notice that the second one includes some improvements. The first resume is good, but most employers would like the additional positive information in the improved resume.

Basic Chronological Resume Example

Everything in this resume supports the candidate's job objective. The emphasis on all related education is important because it helps overcome her lack of extensive work experience.

Judith J. Jones

115 South Hawthorne Avenue
Chicago, Illinois 66204
tel: (312) 653-9217
email: jj@earthlink.com

JOB OBJECTIVE

A position in the office management, accounting, or administrative assistant area that enables me to grow professionally.

EDUCATION AND TRAINING

Acme Business College, Lincoln, IL
Graduate of a one-year business program.

John Adams High School, South Bend, IN
Diploma, business education.

U.S. Army
Financial procedures, accounting functions.

Other: Continuing-education classes and workshops in business communication, spreadsheet and database applications, scheduling systems, and customer relations.

EXPERIENCE

2006–present—Claims Processor, Blue Spear Insurance Co., Wilmette, IL. Process customer medical claims, develop management reports based on created spreadsheets and develop management reports based on those forms, exceed productivity goals.

2005–2006—Returned to school to upgrade business and computer skills. Completed courses in advanced accounting, spreadsheet and database programs, office management, human relations, and new office techniques.

2002–2005—E4, U.S. Army. Assigned to various stations as a specialist in finance operations. Promoted prior to honorable discharge.

2001–2002—Sandy's Boutique, Wilmette, IL. Responsible for counter sales, display design, cash register, and other tasks.

1999–2001—Held part-time and summer jobs throughout high school.

STRENGTHS AND SKILLS

Reliable, hardworking, and good with people. General ledger, accounts payable, and accounts receivable. Proficient in Microsoft Word, WordPerfect, Excel, and Outlook.

Improved Chronological Resume Example

This improved version of the basic resume adds lots of details and specific numbers throughout to reinforce skills.

Judith J. Jones

115 South Hawthorne Avenue
Chicago, IL 66204

jj@earthlink.com
(312) 653-9217 (cell)

JOB OBJECTIVE

A position requiring excellent business management expertise in an office environment. Position should require a variety of skills, including office management, word processing, and spreadsheet and database application use.

EDUCATION AND TRAINING

Acme Business College, Lincoln, IL
Completed one-year program in **Professional Office Management.** Achieved GPA in top 30% of class. Courses included word processing, accounting theory and systems, advanced spreadsheet and database applications, graphics design, time management, and supervision.

John Adams High School, South Bend, IN
Graduated with emphasis on **business courses.** Earned excellent grades in all business topics and won top award for word-processing speed and accuracy.

Other: Continuing-education programs at own expense, including business communications, customer relations, computer applications, and sales techniques.

EXPERIENCE

2006–present—**Claims Processor, Blue Spear Insurance Company,** Wilmette, IL. Process 50 complex medical insurance claims per day, almost 20% above department average. Created a spreadsheet report process that decreased department labor costs by more than $30,000 a year. Received two merit raises for performance.

2005–2006—**Returned to business school to gain advanced office skills.**

2002–2005—**Finance Specialist (E4), U.S. Army.** Systematically processed more than 200 invoices per day from commercial vendors. Trained and supervised eight employees. Devised internal system allowing 15% increase in invoices processed with a decrease in personnel. Managed department with a budget equivalent of more than $350,000 a year. Honorable discharge.

2001–2002—**Sales Associate promoted to Assistant Manager, Sandy's Boutique,** Wilmette, IL. Made direct sales and supervised four employees. Managed daily cash balances and deposits, made purchasing and inventory decisions, and handled all management functions during owner's absence. Sales increased 26% and profits doubled during tenure.

1999–2001—**Held various part-time and summer jobs through high school while maintaining GPA 3.0/4.0.** Earned enough to pay all personal expenses, including car insurance. Learned to deal with customers, meet deadlines, work hard, and handle multiple priorities.

STRENGTHS AND SKILLS

Reliable, with strong work ethic. Excellent interpersonal, written, and oral communication and math skills. Accept supervision well, effectively supervise others, and work well as a team member. General ledger, accounts payable, and accounts receivable expertise. Proficient in Microsoft Word, Excel, PowerPoint, and Outlook; WordPerfect.

Tips for Writing a Simple Chronological Resume

Follow these tips as you write a basic chronological resume:

- **Name:** Use your formal name (not a nickname).

- **Address and contact information:** Avoid abbreviations in your address and include your ZIP code. If you might move, use a friend's address or include a forwarding address. Most employers will not write to you, so provide reliable phone numbers, e-mail addresses, and other contact options. Always include your area code in your phone number because you never know where your resume might travel. Make sure that you have an answering machine or voice mail, and record a professional-sounding message.

- **Job objective/professional summary statement:** You should almost always have one, even if it is general. Notice how Judith Jones keeps her options open with her broad job objective in her basic resume on page 34. Writing "secretary" or "clerical" might limit her from being considered for other jobs. Professional applicants might consider using an impressive summary statement instead, with a heading that states the desired job target.

- **Education and training:** Include any training or education you've had that supports your job objective. If you did not finish a formal degree or program, list what you did complete and emphasize accomplishments. If your experience is not strong, add details here such as related courses and extracurricular activities. In the two examples, Judith Jones puts her business schooling in both the education and experience sections. Doing this fills a job gap and allows her to present her training as equal to work experience.

- **Previous experience:** Include the basics such as employer name, job title, dates employed, and responsibilities—but emphasize specific skills, results, accomplishments, superior performance, and so on.

- **Personal data:** Do not include irrelevant details such as height, weight, and marital status or a photo. Current laws do not allow an employer to base hiring decisions on these points. Providing this information can cause some employers to toss your resume. You can include information about hobbies or leisure activities that directly support your job objective in a special section. The first sample includes a Personal section in which Judith lists some of her strengths, which are often not included in a resume.

- **References:** Make sure that each reference will make nice comments about you and ask each to write a letter of recommendation that you can give to employers. You do not need to list your references on your resume. List them on a separate page and give it to employers who ask.

When you have a simple, errorless, and eye-pleasing resume, get on with your job search. There is no reason to delay! If you want to create a better resume, you can work on improving it in your spare time (evenings or weekends).

Tips for an Improved Chronological Resume

Use these tips to improve your simple resume:

- **Job objective:** A poorly written job objective or summary statement can limit the jobs an employer might consider you for. Think of the skills you have and the types of jobs you want to do; describe them in general terms. Instead of using a narrow job title such as "restaurant manager," you might write "manage a small to mid-sized business."

- **Education and training:** New graduates should emphasize their recent training and education more than those with a few years of related work experience would. A more detailed education and training section might include specific courses you took, and activities or accomplishments that support your job objective or reinforce your key skills. Include other details that reflect how hard you work, such as working your way through school.

- **Skills and accomplishments:** Include those that support your ability to do well in the job you seek now. Even small details count. Maybe your attendance was perfect, you met a tight deadline, or you did the work of others during vacations. Be specific and include numbers—even if you have to estimate them. Judith's improved chronological resume example features a Special Skills and Abilities section and more accomplishments and skills. Notice the impact of the numbers to reinforce results.

- **Job titles:** Past job titles might not accurately reflect what you did. For example, your job title may have been "cashier," but you also opened the store, trained new staff, and covered for the boss on vacations. Perhaps "head cashier and assistant manager" would be more accurate. Check with your previous employer if you are not sure.

- **Promotions:** If you were promoted or got good evaluations, say so—"cashier, promoted to assistant manager," for example. You can list a promotion to a more responsible job as a separate job if doing so results in a stronger resume.

Quip

A resume is not the most effective tool for getting interviews. A better approach is to make direct contact with those who hire or supervise people with your skills and ask them for an interview, even if no openings exist now. Then send a resume.

- **Gaps in employment and other problem areas:** Employee turnover is expensive, so few employers want to hire people who won't stay or who won't work out. Gaps in employment, jobs held for short periods, or a lack of direction in the jobs you've held are all concerns for employers. So consider your situation and try to give an explanation of a problem area. Here are a few examples:

2009—Continued my education at…

2010—Traveled extensively throughout…

2008 to present—Self-employed as barn painter and…

2008—Took year off to have first child

Use entire years to avoid displaying employment gaps you can't explain easily. If you had a few months of unemployment at the beginning of 2008 and then began a job in mid-2008, for example, you can list the job as "2008 to present."

Writing Skills and Combination Resumes

The skills resume emphasizes your most important skills, supported by specific examples of how you have used them. This type of resume allows you to use any part of your life history to support your ability to do the job you want.

While skills resumes can be very effective, creating them requires more work. And some employers don't like them because they can hide a job seeker's faults (such as job gaps, lack of formal education, or little related work experience) better than a chronological resume can. Still, a skills resume may make sense for you.

Look over the sample resumes that follow for ideas. Notice that one resume includes elements of a skills *and* a chronological resume. This so-called combination resume makes sense if your previous job history or education and training are positive.

Put Your Credentials on the Web

These days there are countless options for getting your resume online. If an employer or networking contact asks for your resume, you can give them a URL and let them look at your credentials instantly. One option for an online resume/portfolio with all the bells and whistles is VisualCV (www.visualCV. com). You can include work samples, audio, video, and photos to support your resume details. Another option is to sign up for the business networking site LinkedIn (www.linkedin.com) and fill in the details on your profile. You can then share the profile URL with people who want to know more about your work history.

More Resume Examples

Find resume layout and presentation ideas in the four examples that follow.

 Use the information from your completed Essential Job Search Data Worksheet to write your resume. You can find an online version of this worksheet at www.jist.com/pdf/EJSDW.pdf.

The Chronological Resume to Emphasize Results

This resume focuses on accomplishments through the use of numbers. While Jon's resume does not say so, it is obvious that he works hard and that he gets results.

Jon Feder

2140 Beach Road   Phone: (222) 333-4444
Pompano Beach, Florida 20000   E-mail: jfeder@email.com

Objective	Management position in a major hotel
Summary of Experience	Three years of experience in sales, catering banquet services, and guest relations in a 75-room hotel. Doubled sales revenues from conferences and meetings. Increased dining room and bar revenues by 40%. Won prestigious national and local awards for increased productivity and services.
Experience	Beachcomber Hotel, Pompano Beach, Florida ***Assistant Manager*** 20XX to Present • Oversee a staff of 24, including dining room and bar, housekeeping, and public relations operations. • Introduced new menus and increased dining room revenues by 40%. Awarded *Saveur* magazine's prestigious first place Hotel Cuisine award as a result of my selection of chefs. • Attracted 58% more bar patrons by implementing Friday Night Jazz at the Beach. Tidewater Suites, Hollywood Beach, Florida ***Sales and Public Relations*** 20XX to 20XX • Doubled revenues per month from weddings, conferences, and meetings. • Chosen Chamber of Commerce Newcomer of the Year 20XX for the increase in business within the community.
Education	Associate degree in Hotel Management, Sullivan Technical Institute Certificate in Travel Management, Phoenix University

The Skills Resume for Those with Limited Work Experience

This resume is for a recent high school graduate whose only work experience was at a school office.

Catalina A. Garcia
2340 N. Delaware Street
Denver, Colorado 81613
Cell phone: (413) 123-4567
E-mail: cagarcia@net.net

Position Desired
Office assistant in a fast-paced business

Skills and Abilities

Communication
Excellent written and verbal presentation skills. Use proper grammar and have a good speaking voice.

Interpersonal
Get along well with all types of people. Accept supervision. Helped up to 50 students, visitors, and callers a day in the school office.

Flexible
Willing to try new tasks and am interested in improving efficiency of assigned work.

Attention to Detail
Maintained confidential student records accurately and efficiently.

Hard Working
Worked in the school office during my junior and senior years and maintained above-average grades.

Dependable
Never absent or late in four years.

Award
English Department Student of the Year, May XXXX.

Education

Denver North High School. Graduated in the top 30% of my class. Took advanced English and communication classes. Member of the student newspaper staff for three years.

Girls' basketball team for four years. This activity taught me discipline, teamwork, how to follow instructions, and hard work.

The Combination Resume for Those Changing Careers

This resume emphasizes Grant's relevant education and transferable skills because he has little work experience in the field.

Grant Thomas

717 Carlin Court • Mundelein, IL 60000 • (555) 555-5555 • E-mail: gthomas@aol.com

Profile

- Outstanding student and tutor
- Winner of international computer software design competition three years
- Self-directed and independent, but also a team player
- Effective oral and written communicator
- Creative problem solver

Education and Training

M.S. in Software Engineering, Massachusetts Institute of Technology, Cambridge, MA
B.S. in Computer Engineering, California State University, Fullerton, CA
A rigorous education focusing on topics such as

- Structure and interpretation of computer programs
- Circuits and electronics
- Signals and systems
- Computation structures
- Microelectronic devices and circuits
- Computer system engineering
- Computer language engineering
- Mathematics for computer science
- Analog electronics laboratory
- Digital systems laboratory

Highlights of Experience and Abilities

- Develop, create, and modify general computer applications.
- Analyze user needs and develop software solutions.
- Confer with systems analysts, computer programmers, and others.
- Modify existing software system installation and monitor equipment functioning to ensure specifications are met.
- Supervise work of programmers and technicians.
- Train customers and employees to use new and modified software.

Employment History

Software Specialist, First Rate Computers, Mundelein, IL 20XX to present
- Technician and Customer and Employee Trainer throughout high school
- Promoted to software specialist and worked as a full-time telecommuting employee while completing B.S. and M.S. degrees.

The Electronic Resume

This resume is appropriate for scanning or e-mail submission. It has a plain format that is easily read by scanners. It also has lots of keywords that increase its chances of being selected when an employer searches a database.

```
SAMUEL FEINMAN
489 Smithfield Road
Salem, OR 97301
503.491.3033
samfine@earthlink.net

= = = = = = = = = = = = = = = = = = = = = =

SALES PROFESSIONAL

Dynamic, motivated, award-winning sales professional with extensive
experience. Troubleshooter and problem-solver. Team player who can
motivate self and others. Excellent management and training skills.

= = = = = = = = = = = = = = = = = = = = = =

RELATED EXPERIENCE

Jackson Chevrolet, Springfield, OR
GENERAL MANAGER, XXXX-Present
* Consistently achieve top-ten volume dealer in the Northwest.
* Manage all dealership operations including computer systems, sales,
parts, service, and administration.
* Profitably operate dealership through difficult economic times.
* Meet or exceed customer service, parts, sales, and car service
objectives.
* Maintain high-profile used-car operation.

Afford-A-Ford, Albany, OR
ASSISTANT GENERAL MANAGER, XXXX-XXXX
* Consistently in top five for sales in district; met or exceeded sales
objectives.
* Supervised and trained staff of 90.
* Helped to convert a consistently money-losing store into a profitable
operation by end of first year.
* Focused on customer satisfaction through employee satisfaction and
training.
* Built strong parts and service business, managing excellent
interaction among parts, service, and sales.
* Instituted fleet-sales department and became top fleet-sales dealer
three years running.
* Built lease portfolio from virtually none to 31% of retail.

WetWater Pool Products, Salem, OR
SALES/CUSTOMER SERVICE, XXXX-XXXX
* Advised customers to purchase products that best met their needs while
focusing attention on products more profitable to company.
* Troubleshot and solved customer problems, identifying rapid solutions
and emphasizing customer satisfaction and retention.
* Oversaw shipping and receiving staff.

= = = = = = = = = = = = = = = = = = = = = =

ADDITIONAL EXPERIENCE

State of Oregon, Salem, OR
COMPUTER TECHNICIAN INTERN, XXXX-XXXX
* Built customized computers for state offices.
* Worked with team on installation of computer systems.

= = = = = = = = = = = = = = = = = = = = = =

EDUCATION

AS, Oregon Community College, Troy, OR
Major: Business studies

= = = = = = = = = = = = = = = = = = = = = =

REFERENCES AVAILABLE ON REQUEST
```

Quick Tips for Writing a Cover Letter in 15 Minutes

Whether you're mailing, faxing, or e-mailing your resume, it is important to provide a letter along with your resume that explains why you are sending it—a cover letter (or cover message, in the case of e-mailing). Even when you post your resume in an online database (also known as a resume bank), the Web site where you're posting often has a place where you can upload or paste a cover letter. A cover letter highlights your key qualifications, explains your situation, and asks the recipient for some specific action, consideration, or response.

No matter to whom you are writing, virtually every good cover letter should follow these guidelines.

1. Write to Someone in Particular

Avoid sending a cover letter "To whom it may concern" or using some other impersonal opening. We all get enough junk mail, and if you don't send your letter to someone by name, it will be treated like junk mail.

2. Make Absolutely No Errors

One way to offend people right away is to misspell their names or use incorrect titles. If you are not 100 percent certain, call and verify the correct spelling of the name and other details before you send the letter. Also, review your letters carefully to be sure that they contain no typographical, grammatical, or other errors.

3. Personalize Your Content

No one is impressed by form letters, and you should not use them. Those computer-generated letters that automatically insert a name (known as merge mailings) never fool anyone, and cover letters done in this way are offensive. Small, targeted mailings to a carefully selected group of prospective employers can be effective if you tailor your cover letter to each recipient, but large mass mailings are a waste of time. If you can't customize your letter in some way, don't send it.

4. Present a Good Appearance

Your contacts with prospective employers should always be professional, so buy good-quality stationery and matching envelopes for times when you'll be mailing or hand-delivering a letter and resume. Use papers and envelopes that match or complement your resume paper. The standard 8 1/2 × 11 paper size is typically used, but you can also use the smaller Monarch-size paper with matching envelopes. For colors, use white, ivory, or light beige—whatever matches your resume paper. Employers expect cover letters to be word processed and produced with excellent print quality.

Use a standard letter format that complements your resume type and format. You might find it easier to use your word-processing software's template functions than to create a format from scratch. Your letters don't have to be fancy; they do have to look professional. And don't forget the envelope! It should be typed and printed carefully, without errors.

You will send many of your cover letters as e-mail messages. All the rules for traditional cover letters apply equally to e-mail cover letters. Just because e-mail is a less formal means of communicating doesn't mean you can be careless with writing, spelling, grammar, punctuation, or presentation. But e-mail letters should be shorter and crisper than traditional paper letters.

5. Begin with a Friendly Opening

Start your letter by sharing the reason you are writing and, if appropriate, a reminder of any prior contacts or the name of the person who referred you. See the examples on pages 46 and 47 for ideas for beginning your letters.

6. Target Your Skills and Experiences

To effectively target your skills and experiences, you must know something about the organization, the job opportunity, or the person with whom you are dealing. Present any relevant background that may be of particular interest to the person to whom you are writing.

7. Close with an Action Statement

Don't close your letter without clearly identifying what you will do next. Don't leave it up to the employer to contact you, because that doesn't guarantee a response. Close on a positive note and let the employer know how and when you will be following up.

Sample Printed Cover Letter

Allan P. Raymond, CPA

29 Brookside Drive, Mystic, CT 06433
860.239.7671 • allanraymond@verizon.net

March 15, 20XX

Carol P. Graves, CPA
President, Graves & Andrews
254 Court Street
New London, CT 06320

Dear Carol:

I enjoyed our conversation at the recent CPA Society meeting and, as you suggested, I am forwarding my resume with this letter of interest in joining your firm.

You and I agreed that your clients deserve the best: the best accountants, the best strategies, and the greatest dedication to customer service. I am confident I can bring "the best" in both attitude and execution to your firm.

With more than ten years of accounting experience—the last five as a CPA and owner of an accounting firm specializing in tax—I have strong and well-proven professional skills. I thrive on the challenges and intricacies of tax accounting and stay up-to-date with tax code changes through both in-person and online training programs.

What satisfies me most in my professional life is the opportunity to help clients better manage, control, and benefit from their money. One of the keys to the good advice I give my clients is my deep understanding of the consequences of investment decisions on their tax situation. I have worked with businesses of all sizes—from one person to complex multimillion-dollar organizations—in diverse industries and have contributed strategies and planning recommendations as well as tax-related accounting services.

Having just concluded the sale of my business, I am eager for new professional challenges. I would like to explore my value as a tax accountant with your firm, and in pursuit of that objective I will call you next week to schedule a meeting. Thank you.

Best regards,

Allan P. Raymond

enclosure: resume

Written by Louise Kursmark

Sample E-mail Cover Letter

Dear Ms. Gold:

My sister, Tracy Oswald, tells me that you are looking for a systems administrator for your growing San Francisco operation.

I am experienced, reliable, loyal, and customer focused and would like to talk with you about joining your team.

The enclosed resume describes nearly 15 years of experience with Anthem Blue Cross/Blue Shield, during which I advanced to increasingly responsible technical positions. Whether independently or with a team, I worked hard to provide the best possible service and support to my "customers." I was recognized for my strong technical skills, ability to guide less experienced support people, and 100% reliability.

A recent downsizing at Anthem caused my position to be eliminated, and I am looking for a new opportunity with a company like yours, where my technical abilities, positive attitude, and dedication will be valued.

I will call you next week in hopes of getting together soon.

Yours truly,

Kevin Oswald

****
Attachment: resume

Written by Louise Kursmark

STEP 5: Organize Your Time to Get Two Interviews a Day

The average job seeker gets about five interviews a month—fewer than two a week. Yet many job seekers use the methods in this *Quick Job Search* to get two interviews a day. Getting two interviews a day equals 10 a week and 40 a month. That's 800 percent more interviews than the average job seeker gets. Who do you think will get a job offer quicker?

You might think that getting two interviews a day sounds impossible. However, getting two interviews a day is quite possible if you redefine what counts as an interview and use the networking techniques from step 3.

The New Definition of an Interview: Any face-to-face contact with someone who has the authority to hire or supervise a person with your skills—even if no opening exists at the time you talk with them.

If you use this new definition, it becomes *much* easier to get interviews. You can now interview with all sorts of potential employers, not just those who have job openings now. While most other job seekers look for advertised or actual openings, you can get interviews before a job opens up or before it is advertised and widely known. You will be considered for jobs that may soon be created but that others will not know about. And, of course, you can also interview for existing openings just as everyone else does.

Spending as much time as possible on your job search and setting a job search schedule are important parts of this step. Researchers at the University of Missouri found in a 2009 study that developing and following a job search plan from the start, as well as having a positive attitude about your search, had a significant impact on job search success (*U.S. News & World Report*, September 24, 2009).

Make Your Search a Full-Time Job

Job seekers average fewer than 15 hours a week looking for work. On average, unemployment lasts three or more months, with some people out of work far longer (for example, older workers and higher earners). My many years of experience researching job seeking indicate that the more time you spend on your job search each week, the less time you will likely remain unemployed.

Of course, using the more effective job search methods presented in this book also helps. Many job search programs that teach job seekers my basic approach of using more effective methods and spending more time looking have proven that these seekers often find a job in half the average time. More importantly, many job seekers also find better jobs using these methods.

So, if you are unemployed and looking for a full-time job, you should plan to look on a full-time basis. It just makes sense to do so, although many do not, or they start out well but quickly get discouraged. Most job seekers simply don't have a structured plan—they have no idea what they are going to do next Thursday. The plan that follows will show you how to structure your job search like a job.

Decide How Much Time You Will Spend Looking for Work Each Week and Day

First and most importantly, decide how many hours you are willing to spend each week on your job search. You should spend a minimum of 25 hours a week on hardcore job search activities with no goofing around. The following worksheet walks you through a simple but effective process to set a job search schedule for each week.

PLAN YOUR JOB SEARCH WEEK

1. How many hours are you willing to spend each week looking for a job? _____

   _____

2. Which days of the week will you spend looking for a job?

   _____

   _____

3. How many hours will you look each day? _____

   _____

4. At what times will you begin and end your job search on each of these days? _____

   _____

Create a Specific Daily Job Search Schedule

Having a specific daily schedule is essential because most job seekers find it hard to stay productive each day. The sample daily schedule that follows is the result of years of research into what schedule gets the best results. I tested many schedules in job search programs I ran, and this particular schedule worked best.

Consider using a schedule like this sample daily schedule. Why? Because it works.

A Sample Daily Schedule That Works

Time	Activity
7–8 a.m.	Get up, shower, dress, eat breakfast.
8–8:15 a.m.	Organize workspace, review schedule for today's interviews and promised follow-ups, check e-mail, and update schedule as needed.
8:15–9 a.m.	Review old leads for follow-up needed today; develop new leads from want ads, yellow pages, the Internet, warm contact lists, and other sources; complete daily contact list.
9–10 a.m.	Make phone calls and set up interviews.
10–10:15 a.m.	Take a break.
10:15–11 a.m.	Make more phone calls; set up more interviews.
11 a.m.–Noon	Send follow-up notes and do other office activities as needed.
Noon–1 p.m.	Lunch break, relax.
1–3 p.m.	Go on interviews; make cold contacts in the field.
Evening	Read job search books, make calls to warm contacts not reachable during the day, work on a better resume, spend time with friends and family, exercise, relax.

If you are not accustomed to using a daily schedule book or electronic planner, promise yourself to get a good one today. Choose one that allows for each day's plan on an hourly basis, plus daily to-do lists. Record your daily schedule in advance, and then add interviews as they come. Get used to carrying your planner with you and use it!

You can find a variety of computer programs and smartphone apps to help organize your job search. An example of a Web site that offers a free job search planning system online is JibberJobber (www.jibberjobber.com).

STEP 6: Dramatically Improve Your Interviewing Skills

Interviews are where the job search action is. You have to get them; then you have to do well in them. According to surveys of employers, most job seekers do not effectively present the skills they have to do the job. Even worse, most job seekers can't answer one or more problem questions.

This lack of performance in interviews is one reason why employers will often hire a job seeker who does well in the interview over someone with better credentials. The good news is that you can do simple things to dramatically improve your interviewing skills. This section emphasizes interviewing tips and techniques that make the most difference.

Your First Impression May Be the Only One You Make

Some research suggests that if the interviewer forms a negative impression in the first five minutes of an interview, your chances of getting a job offer approach zero. I know from experience that many job seekers can create a lasting negative impression within seconds.

Tips for Interviewing

Because a positive first impression is so important, I share these suggestions to help you get off to a good start:

- **Make a good impression before you arrive.** Your resume, e-mails, applications, and other written correspondence create an impression before the interview, so make them professional and error free.

- **Do some homework on the organization before you go.** You can often get information on a business and on industry trends from the Internet or a library.

- **Dress and groom the same way the interviewer is likely to be dressed—but better!** Employer surveys find that almost half of all people's dress or grooming creates an initial negative impression. So this is a big problem. If necessary, get advice on your interviewing outfits from someone who dresses well. Pay close attention to your grooming, too—little things do count.

- **Be early.** Leave in plenty of time to be a few minutes early to an interview.

(continued)

(continued)

- **Be friendly and respectful with the receptionist.** Doing otherwise will often get back to the interviewer and result in a quick rejection.

- **Follow the interviewer's lead in the first few minutes.** The interview often begins with informal small talk, but the interviewer uses this time to see how you interact. This is a good time to make a positive comment on the organization or even something you see in the office.

- **Understand that a traditional interview is not a friendly exchange.** In a traditional interview situation, there is a job opening, and you will be one of several applicants for it. In this setting, the employer's task is to eliminate all applicants but one. The interviewer's questions are designed to elicit information that can be used to screen you out. And your objective is to avoid getting screened out. It's hardly an open and honest interaction, is it?

  Setting up interviews before an opening exists eliminates the stress of a traditional interview. In pre-interviews, employers are not trying to screen you out, and you are not trying to keep them from finding out stuff about you. Having said that, knowing how to answer questions that might be asked in a traditional interview is good preparation for any interview you face.

- **Be prepared to answer the tough interview questions.** Your answers to a few key problem questions may determine whether you get a job offer. There are simply too many possible interview questions to cover one by one. Instead, 10 basic questions cover variations of most other interview questions. So, if you can learn to answer the Top 10 Problem Interview Questions well, you will know how to answer most others.

- **Be prepared for the most important interview question of all.** "Why should I hire you?" is the most important question of all to answer well. Do you have a convincing argument why someone should hire you over someone else? If you don't, you probably won't get that job you really want. So think carefully about why someone should hire you and practice your response. Then make sure you communicate this in the interview, even if the interviewer never asks the question in a clear way.

Top 10 Problem Interview Questions

1. Why should I hire you?
2. Why don't you tell me about yourself?
3. What are your major strengths?
4. What are your major weaknesses?
5. What sort of pay do you expect to receive?
6. How does your previous experience relate to the jobs we have here?

7. What are your plans for the future?

8. What will your former employer (or references) say about you?

9. Why are you looking for this type of position, and why here?

10. Why don't you tell me about your personal situation?

Follow the Three-Step Process for Answering Interview Questions

I've developed a three-step process for answering interview questions. I know this might seem too simple, but the three-step process is easy to remember and can help you create a good answer to most interview questions. The technique has worked for thousands of people, so consider trying it.

1. **Understand what is really being asked.** Most questions are designed to find out about your self-management skills and personality, but interviewers are rarely this blunt. The employer's *real* question is often one or more of the following:

   - Can I depend on you?

   - Are you easy to get along with?

   - Are you a good worker?

   - Do you have the experience and training to do the job if we hire you?

   - Are you likely to stay on the job for a reasonable period of time and be productive?

   Ultimately, if you don't convince the employer that you will stay and be a good worker, it won't matter if you have the best credentials—he or she won't hire you.

2. **Answer the question briefly in a nondamaging way.** Present the facts of your particular work experience as advantages, not disadvantages. Many interview questions encourage you to provide negative information. One classic question in the list of Top 10 Problem Interview Questions is "What are your major weaknesses?" This is obviously a trick question, and many people are just not prepared for it.

   A good response is to mention something that is not very damaging, such as "I have been told that I am a perfectionist, sometimes not delegating as effectively as I might." But your answer is not complete until you continue with the next step.

3. **Answer the real question by presenting your related skills.** Base your answer on the key skills you have that support the job, and give examples to support these skills. For example, an employer might say to a recent graduate, "We were looking for someone with more experience in this field. Why should we consider you?" Here is one possible answer:

"I'm sure there are people who have more experience, but I do have more than six years of work experience, including three years of advanced training and hands-on experience using the latest methods and techniques. Because my training is recent, I am open to new ideas and am used to working hard and learning quickly."

In the previous example (about your need to delegate), a good skills statement might be

"I've been working on this problem and have learned to let my staff do more, making sure that they have good training and supervision. I've found that their performance improves, and it frees me up to do other things."

Whatever your situation, learn to answer questions in ways that present you well. It's essential to communicate your skills during an interview, and the three-step process can help you answer problem questions and dramatically improve your responses. It works!

How to Earn a Thousand Dollars a Minute

What do you do when the employer asks, "How much money would it take to get you to join our company?"

Tips on Negotiating Pay

Remember these few essential tips when it comes time to negotiate your pay:

- **The #1 Salary Negotiation Rule: The person who names a specific amount first loses.**
- **The only time to negotiate is after you have been offered the job.** Employers want to know how much you want to be paid so that they can eliminate you from consideration. They figure if you want too much, you won't be happy with the job and won't stay. And if you will take too little, they may think you don't have enough experience. So never discuss your salary expectations until an employer offers you the job.
- **If pressed, speak in terms of wide pay ranges.** If you are pushed to reveal your pay expectations early in an interview, ask the interviewer what the normal pay range is for this job. Interviewers will often tell you, and you can say that you would consider offers in this range.

If you are forced to be more specific, speak in terms of a wide pay range. If you figure that the company will likely pay from $25,000 to $29,000 a year, for example, say that you would consider "any fair offer in the mid-twenties to low thirties." This statement covers the employer's range and goes a bit higher. If all else fails, tell the interviewer that you would consider any reasonable offer.

For this tip to work, you must know in advance what the job is likely to pay. You can get this information by asking people who do similar work, or from a variety of books and Internet sources of career information, such as the *Occupational Outlook Handbook* (www.bls.gov/oco) or Salary.com.

- **If you want the job, you should say so.** This is no time to be playing games.
- **Don't say "no" too quickly.** Never, ever turn down a job offer during an interview! Instead, thank the interviewer for the offer and ask to consider the offer overnight. You can turn it down tomorrow, saying how much you appreciate the offer and asking to be considered for other jobs that pay better. And it is okay to ask for additional pay or other concessions. But if you simply can't accept the offer, say why and ask the interviewer to keep you in mind for future opportunities. You just never know.

 # STEP 7: Follow Up on All Job Leads

It's a fact: People who follow up with potential employers and with others in their network get jobs more quickly than those who do not.

Rules for Effective Follow-Up

Here are four rules to guide you in following up in your job search:

- **Send a thank-you note or e-mail to every person who helps you in your job search.**
- **Send the note within 24 hours after speaking with the person.**
- **Enclose JIST Cards with thank-you notes and all other correspondence.**
- **Develop a system to keep following up with good contacts.**

Thank-You Notes Make a Difference

Although thank-you notes can be e-mailed, most people appreciate and are more impressed by a mailed note. Here are some tips about mailed thank-you notes that you can easily adapt to e-mail use:

- You can handwrite or type thank-you notes on quality paper and matching envelopes.
- Keep the notes simple, neat, and error free.
- Make sure to include a few copies of your JIST Card in the envelope.

Following is an example of a simple thank-you note.

April 5, XXXX

M. Kijek,

Thanks so much for your willingness to see me next Wednesday at 9 a.m. I know that I am one of many who are interested in working with your organization. I appreciate the opportunity to meet you and learn more about the position.

I've enclosed a JIST Card that presents the basics of my skills for this job and will bring my resume to the interview. Please call me if you have any questions at all.

Sincerely,

Bruce Vernon

Use Job Lead Cards to Follow Up

If you use contact management software or an app on your phone, use it to schedule follow-up activities. But the simple paper system I describe here can work very well or can be adapted for setting up your contact management software.

- Use a simple 3-by-5-inch card to record essential information about each person in your network.

- Buy a 3-by-5-inch card file box and tabs for each day of the month.

- File the cards under the date you want to contact the person.

- Follow through by contacting the person on that date.

I've found that staying in touch with a good contact every other week can pay off big. Here's a sample card to give you ideas about creating your own.

ORGANIZATION: _Mutual Health Insurance_

CONTACT PERSON: _Anna Tomey_　　　　PHONE: _317-355-0216_

SOURCE OF LEAD: _Aunt Ruth_

NOTES: _4/10 Called. Anna on vacation. Call back 4/15. 4/15 Interview set 4/20 at 1:30. 4/20 Anna showed me around. They use the same computers we used in school! (Friendly people.) Sent thank-you note and JIST Card, call back 5/1. 5/1 Second interview 5/8 at 9 a.m.!_

In Closing

This is a short book, but it may be all you need to get a better job in less time. I hope this will be true for you, and I wish you well in your search. Remember this: You won't get a job offer because someone knocks on your door and offers one. Job seeking does involve luck, but you are more likely to have good luck if you are out getting interviews.

I'll close this book with a few final tips:

- **Approach your job search as if it were a job itself.** Create and stick to a daily schedule, and spend at least 25 hours a week looking.

- **Follow up on each lead you generate and ask each contact for referrals.**

- **Set out each day to schedule at least two interviews.** Remember the new definition of an interview—an interview can just be talking to a potential employer that doesn't have an opening now but might in the future.

- **Send out lots of thank-you notes and JIST Cards.**

- **When you want the job, tell the employer that you want it and why you should be hired over everyone else.**

Don't get discouraged. There are lots of jobs out there, and someone needs an employee with your skills—your job is to find that someone.

I wish you luck in your job search and in your life.

Appendix A

(continued)

(continued)

Accomplishments/things you did well _____

_____

_____

Specific things you can do as a result _____

_____

_____

Schools you attended after high school, specific years attended, and degrees/certificates earned _____

_____

_____

Courses related to job objective _____

_____

_____

Related extracurricular activities/hobbies/leisure activities _____

_____

_____

Accomplishments/things you did well _____

_____

_____

Specific things you can do as a result _____

_____

_____

Other Training

Include formal or informal learning, workshops, military training, skills you learned on the job or from hobbies—anything that will help support your job objective. Include specific dates, certificates earned, or other details as needed. _____

_____

_____

Work and Volunteer History

List your most recent job first, followed by each previous job. Military experience, unpaid or volunteer work, and work in a family business should be included here, too. If needed, use additional sheets to cover *all* significant paid or unpaid work experiences. Emphasize details that will help support your new job objective. Include numbers to support what you did: the number of people served over one or more years, number of transactions processed, percentage of sales increased, total inventory value you were responsible for, payroll of the staff you supervised, total budget responsible for, and so on. Emphasize results you achieved, using numbers to support them whenever possible. Mentioning these things on your resume and in an interview will help you get the job you want.

Job 1

Dates employed _____

Name of organization _____

Supervisor's name and job title _____

Address _____

_____

Phone number/e-mail address/Web site _____

_____

What did you accomplish and do well? _____

_____

(continued)

(continued)

Things you learned; skills you developed or used _____

_____

_____

Raises, promotions, positive evaluations, awards _____

_____

_____

Computer software, hardware, and other equipment you used _____

_____

_____

Other details that might support your job objective _____

_____

_____

Job 2

Dates employed _____

Name of organization _____

Supervisor's name and job title _____

Address _____

_____

Phone number/e-mail address/Web site _____

_____

What did you accomplish and do well? _____

_____

_____

Things you learned; skills you developed or used _____

_____

_____

Raises, promotions, positive evaluations, awards_____

_____

_____

Computer software, hardware, and other equipment you used_____

_____

_____

Other details that might support your job objective_____

_____

_____

Job 3

Dates employed_____

Name of organization_____

Supervisor's name and job title_____

Address_____

_____

Phone number/e-mail address/Web site_____

_____

What did you accomplish and do well?_____

_____

_____

Things you learned; skills you developed or used_____

_____

_____

Raises, promotions, positive evaluations, awards_____

_____

_____

(continued)

(continued)

Computer software, hardware, and other equipment you used_____

_____

_____

Other details that might support your job objective_____

_____

_____

References

Think of people who know your work well and will be positive about your work and character. Past supervisors are best. Contact them and tell them what type of job you want and your qualifications, and ask what they will say about you if contacted by a potential employer. Some employers will not provide references by phone, so ask them for a letter of reference in advance. If a past employer may say negative things, negotiate what they will say or get written references from others you worked with there.

Reference name_____

Position or title_____

Relationship to you_____

Contact information (complete address, phone number, e-mail address)

_____

_____

Reference name_____

Position or title_____

Relationship to you_____

Contact information (complete address, phone number, e-mail address)

_____

_____

Reference name _____

Position or title _____

Relationship to you _____

Contact information (complete address, phone number, e-mail address)

_____

_____

Appendix B

Additional Resources

Thousands of books and countless Internet sites provide information on career subjects. Space limitations do not permit me to describe the many good resources available, so I list here some of the most useful ones. Because this is my list, I've included books I've written or that JIST publishes. You should be able to find these and many other resources at libraries, bookstores, and Web bookselling sites such as Amazon.com.

Resume and Cover Letter Books

My books: *The Quick Resume & Cover Letter Book* is one of the top-selling resume books. It is very simple to follow and has good sample resumes written by professional resume writers. For more in-depth but still quick help, check out my two books in the *Help in a Hurry* series: *Same-Day Resume* (with advice on creating a simple resume in an hour and a better one later) and *15-Minute Cover Letter,* co-authored with Louise Kursmark (offering sample cover letters and tips for writing them fast and effectively).

Other books published by JIST: The following titles include many sample resumes written by professional resume writers, as well as good advice: *Amazing Resumes* by Jim Bright and Joanne Earl; *Cover Letter Magic* by Wendy S. Enelow and Louise M. Kursmark; the entire *Expert Resumes* series by Enelow and Kursmark; *Federal Resume Guidebook* by Kathryn Kraemer Troutman; *Gallery of Best Resumes, Gallery of Best Cover Letters,* and other books by David F. Noble; *Résumé Magic* by Susan Britton Whitcomb; *30-Minute Resume Makeover* by Louise Kursmark; and *Step-by-Step Resumes* by Evelyn Salvador.

Job Search and Interviewing Books

My books: You may want to check out my book in the *Help in a Hurry* series *Next-Day Job Interview* (quick tips for preparing for a job interview at the last minute). *The Very Quick Job Search* is a thorough book with detailed advice and a "quick" section of key tips you can finish in a few hours. *Getting the Job You Really Want* includes many in-the-book activities and good career decision-making and job search advice.

Other books published by JIST: *Job Search Magic, Interview Magic,* and *The Christian's Career Journey* by Susan Britton Whitcomb; *Make Job Loss Work for You* by Richard and Terri Deems; *Military-to-Civilian Career Transition*

Guide by Janet Farley; *Your Dream Job Game Plan* by Molly Fletcher; *Ultimate Job Search* by Richard H. Beatty; *The Career Coward's Guide* series by Katy Piotrowski; and *The Twitter Job Search Guide* by Susan Britton Whitcomb, Chandlee Bryan, and Deb Dib.

Books with Information on Jobs

JIST's primary reference books: The *Occupational Outlook Handbook* is the source of job titles listed in this book. Published by the U.S. Department of Labor and updated every other year, the *OOH* covers about 90 percent of the workforce. The *O*NET Dictionary of Occupational Titles* book has descriptions for 950 jobs based on the O*NET (Occupational Information Network) database developed by the Department of Labor. The *Enhanced Occupational Outlook Handbook* includes the *OOH* descriptions plus more than 5,600 additional descriptions of related jobs from the O*NET and other sources. The *New Guide for Occupational Exploration* allows you to explore major jobs based on your interests.

Other books published by JIST: Here are a few good books that include job descriptions and helpful details on career options: *Best Jobs for the 21ˢᵗ Century, 50 Best Jobs for Your Personality, 150 Best Recession-Proof Jobs, 40 Best Fields for Your Career, 200 Best Jobs for College Graduates,* and *300 Best Jobs Without a Four-Year Degree.* These books include selected jobs from the *OOH* and other information: The *Top Careers* series and *Overnight Career Choice.*

Internet Resources

There are too many Web sites to list, but here are a few places you can start. A book by Anne Wolfinger titled *Best Career and Education Web Sites* gives unbiased reviews of the most helpful sites and ideas on how to use them. *Job Seeker's Online Goldmine,* by Janet Wall, lists the extensive free online job search tools from government and other sources. The *Occupational Outlook Handbook's* job descriptions also include Internet addresses for related organizations. And www.jist.com lists recommended sites for career, education, and related topics, along with comments on each. Be aware that some Web sites provide poor advice, so ask your librarian, instructor, or counselor for suggestions on those best for your needs.

Other Resources

Libraries: Most libraries have the books mentioned here, as well as many other resources. Many also provide Internet access so that you can research online information. Ask the librarian for help with finding what you need.

People: People who hold the jobs that interest you are among the best career information sources. Ask them what they like and don't like about their work, how they got started, and the education or training needed. Most people are helpful and will give advice you can't get any other way.

Career counseling: A good vocational counselor can help you explore career options. Take advantage of this service if it is available to you! Also consider a career-planning course or program, which will encourage you to be more thorough in your thinking.

Appendix C

Use a Career Portfolio to Support Your Resume

Your resume is impressive, but there is another way that you can show prospective employers evidence of who you are and what you can do: a career portfolio.

What Is a Career Portfolio?

Unlike a resume, a career portfolio is a collection of documents that can include a variety of items. Here are some items you may want to place in your portfolio:

- Resume.

- School transcripts.

- Summary of skills.

- Credentials, such as diplomas and certificates of recognition.

- Reference letters from school officials and instructors, former employers, or coworkers.

- List of accomplishments: Describe hobbies and interests that are not directly related to your job objective and are not included on your resume.

- Examples of your work: Depending on your situation, you can include samples of your art, photographs of a project, audio, video, images of Web pages you developed, and other media that can provide examples of your work.

Place each item on a separate page when you assemble your career portfolio.

Create a Digital Portfolio

A digital portfolio, also known as an electronic portfolio, contains all the information from your career portfolio in an electronic format. This material is then copied onto a CD-ROM or published on a Web site. With a digital portfolio, you can present your skills to a greater number of people than you can your paper career portfolio. VisualCV (www.visualcv.com) one site that helps you build a digital portfolio and post it online.

YOUR CAREER PORTFOLIO

On the following lines, list the items you want to include in your career portfolio. Think specifically of those items that show your skills, education, and personal accomplishments.

_____

_____

_____

_____

_____

_____

_____

_____

_____

_____

_____

_____

_____

_____

_____

_____

_____

_____

_____

_____

NOTES

NOTES

NOTES

NOTES

NOTES

NOTES